SandCastle™
Let's Measure

WHAT
in the
WORLD
is a
POUND?

Mary Elizabeth Salzmann

Published by ABDO Publishing Company, 8000 West 78th Street, Edina, Minnesota 55439.
Copyright © 2009 by Abdo Consulting Group, Inc. International copyrights reserved in all countries.
No part of this book may be reproduced in any form without written permission from the publisher.
SandCastle™ is a trademark and logo of ABDO Publishing Company.

Printed in the United States of America, North Mankato, Minnesota.
012009 072011

Editor: Pam Price
Curriculum Coordinator: Nancy Tuminelly
Cover and Interior Design and Production: Colleen Dolphin, Mighty Media
Photo Credits: Colleen Dolphin, Eyewire Images, Shutterstock
Illustrations: Colleen Dolphin

Library of Congress Cataloging-in-Publication Data

Salzmann, Mary Elizabeth, 1968-

What in the world is a pound? / Mary Elizabeth Salzmann.

p. cm. -- (Let's measure)

ISBN 978-1-60453-165-7

1. Volume (Cubic content)--Juvenile literature. 2. Measurement--Juvenile literature.
3. Weights and measures--Juvenile literature. I. Title.

QC104.S356 2009

530.8'13--dc22

2008005486

SandCastle™ books are created by a professional team of educators, reading specialists, and content developers around five essential components—phonemic awareness, phonics, vocabulary, text comprehension, and fluency—to assist young readers as they develop reading skills and strategies and increase their general knowledge. All books are written, reviewed, and leveled for guided reading, early reading intervention, and Accelerated Reader® programs for use in shared, guided, and independent reading and writing activities to support a balanced approach to literacy instruction. The SandCastle™ series has four levels that correspond to early literacy development in young children. The levels are provided to help teachers and parents select appropriate books for young readers.

SandCastle Level: Transitional

Emerging Readers
(no flags)

Beginning Readers
(1 flag)

Transitional Readers
(2 flags)

Fluent Readers
(3 flags)

SandCastle™ would like to hear from you! Please send us your comments or questions.

sandcastle@abdopublishing.com

www.abdopublishing.com

A pound is a unit of measurement. Pounds are used to measure weight. A football weighs about 1 pound.

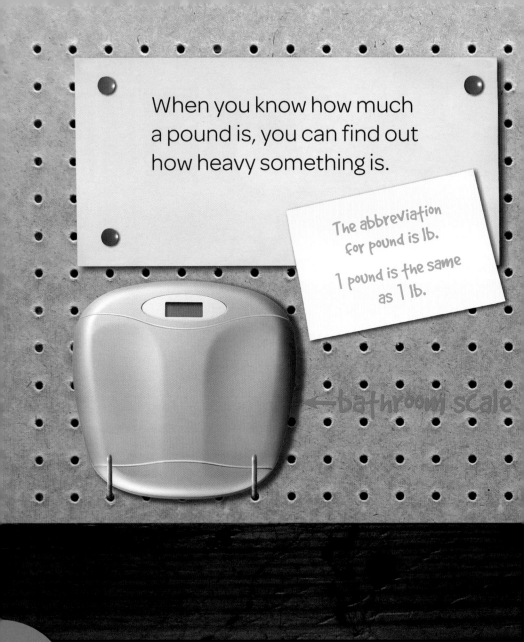

When you know how much a pound is, you can find out how heavy something is.

The abbreviation for pound is lb.

1 pound is the same as 1 lb.

←bathroom scale

A scale is the tool you use to measure weight. There are different kinds of scales. Measuring weight is also called weighing.

kitchen scale

OUNCES

ALLISON CAN MEASURE!

Allison likes to play many different sports. She wants to find out how much some of her sports equipment weighs.

First she measures the weight of her red bowling ball. It weighs 9 pounds.

SALTER

9

Then Allison weighs her hockey helmet. It weighs 3 pounds.

SALTER

3

Next she weighs her hockey skates. They weigh 5 pounds.

Allison weighs her skateboard.
It weighs 6 pounds.

She weighs her softball bat.
It weighs 1 pound.

Finally Allison weighs her snorkeling gear. It weighs 3 pounds.

1 lb.

6 lbs.

Allison puts her sports equipment in order from lightest to heaviest.

3 lbs.

3 lbs.

5 lbs.

9 lbs.

MEASURING EVERY DAY!

Luke took Cuddles
to the vet for a checkup.
The vet weighed Cuddles.
She weighs 5 pounds.

5

At the pumpkin patch, Blake weighs the pumpkin before he buys it. The pumpkin weighs 15 pounds.

15

Katie holds her mom's dumbbells.
Each dumbbell weighs 2 pounds.
Together they weigh 4 pounds.
(2 + 2 = 4)

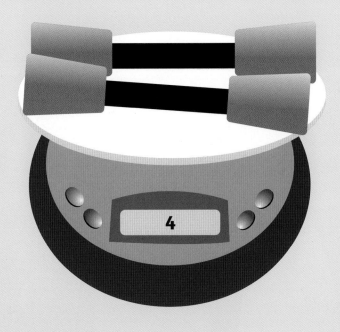

Before school, Matt and Deb weigh their backpacks. They want to see whose is heaviest. Matt's backpack weighs 5 pounds. Deb's weighs 8 pounds

MEASURING IS FUN!

How many pounds do you weigh?
What else can you measure in pounds?

LET'S MEASURE!

Which of these things is about one pound?

MORE ABOUT MEASURING

Weight

16 ounces = 1 pound

Sometimes you use both pounds and ounces to weigh something.

The book weighs 1 pound and 4 ounces. This can also be written 1 lb. 4 oz.

GLOSSARY

abbreviation – a short way to write a word.

checkup – a routine exam by a doctor.

dumbbell – a short bar that is heavier at the ends and is used for exercise.

equipment – a set of tools or items used for a special purpose or activity.

snorkel – to swim underwater while breathing through a long tube.

unit – an amount used as a standard of measurement.

vet – a doctor who takes care of animals; *vet* is short for *veterinarian*.